D1710860

Special thanks to Mike Burton (California State University-East Bay) and all the incredibly helpful librarians throughout the Golden State.—H.A.

To Marc, Rocket, and Gidget—can't wait for our roadtrip!.—J.T.

First published in 2022 by Wide Eyed Editions, an imprint of The Quarto Group.
100 Cummings Center, Suite 265D, Beverly, MA 01915, USA. T +1 978-282-9590
F +1 078-283-2742 www.Quarto.com

A CIP record for this book is available from the Library of Congress.

ISBN 978-0-7112-7404-4

The illustrations were created digitally
Set in Quicksand and Thirsty Script

Published by Georgia Amson-Bradshaw
Designed by Myrto Dimitrakoulia
Edited by Hattie Grylls
Production by Dawn Cameron

Manufactured in Guangdong, China TT052022

9 8 7 6 5 4 3 2 1

Only in California

Written by **Heather Alexander** · Illustrated by **Jen Taylor**

WIDE EYED EDITIONS

Contents

Welcome to California

Hop in the (imaginary) car 'cause we're going on a wacky road trip to experience all the WEIRD and WONDERFUL things this amazing and super-sized state has to offer. I mean, where else can you go surfing, skiing, to a movie premiere, and to a garlic festival all on the same day? Open the rooftop (we're rocking a convertible 'cause, hello, California sunshine!) and soak in the salty beauty of palm tree-lined beaches. Farther north, as the fog descends, lush forests, glimmering lakes, snowy mountain peaks, and national parks with sky-high sequoias and redwoods make us gasp in awe. And when we circle back southeast, we're greeted by the stark splendor of the scorching desert. As we travel, we'll highlight the offbeat, amazing, and just plain weird history, buildings, attractions, festivals, plants, animals, and people that make California uniquely California.

A pine tree and palm tree were planted next to each other on Highway 99 near Madera to symbolize the meeting point of Northern and Southern California, but the state's GEOGRAPHIC CENTER sits between North Fork and Italian Bar.

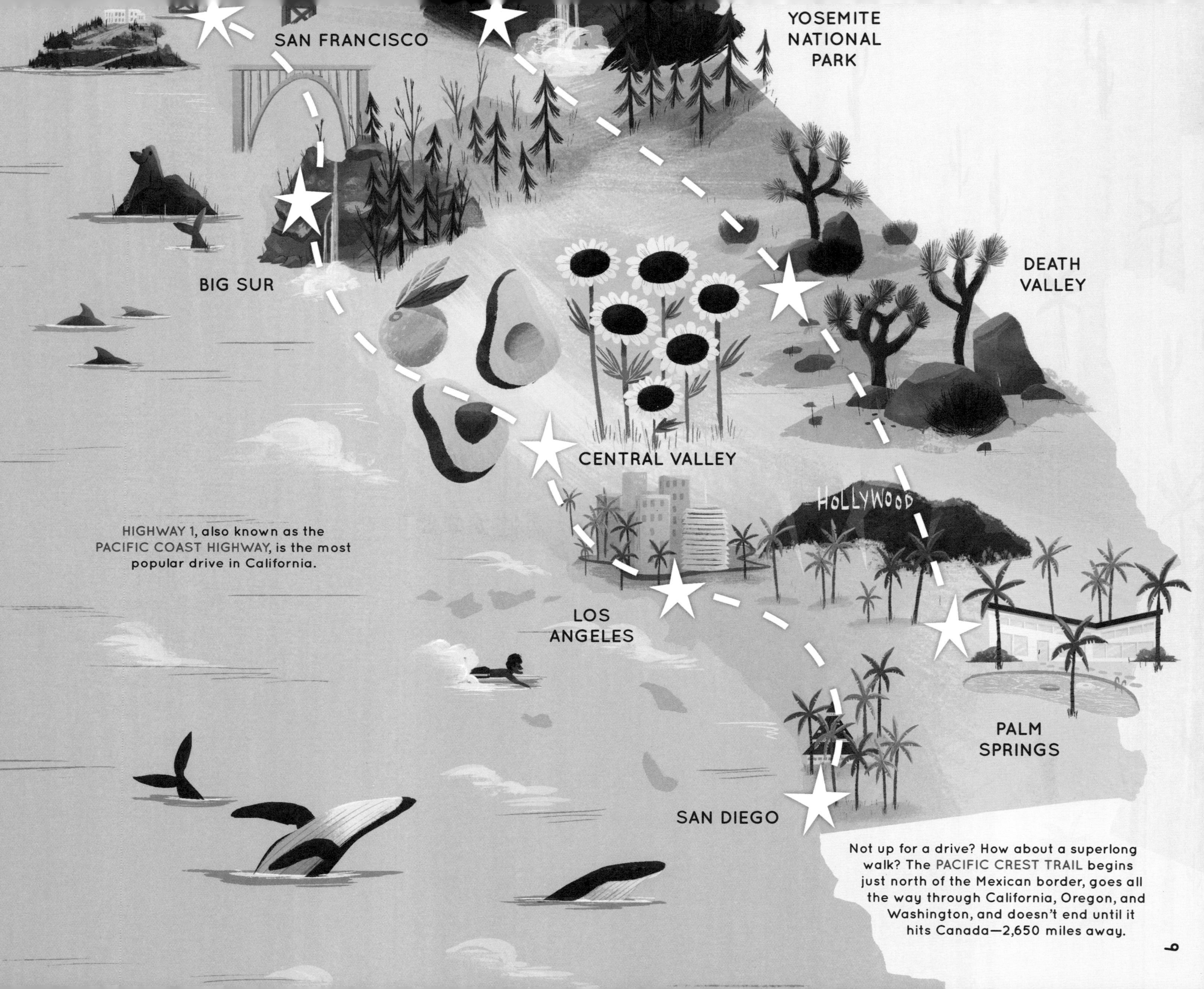

HIGHWAY 1, also known as the PACIFIC COAST HIGHWAY, is the most popular drive in California.

Not up for a drive? How about a superlong walk? The PACIFIC CREST TRAIL begins just north of the Mexican border, goes all the way through California, Oregon, and Washington, and doesn't end until it hits Canada—2,650 miles away.

BALBOA PARK is even bigger than New York City's Central Park! Do you have the skills to grab the brass ring as you spin on the historic CAROUSEL built in 1910?

Every year, more than a 100,000 megafans attend COMIC-CON INTERNATIONAL dressed as their favorite characters. Which character would you be?

The SAN DIEGO-CORONADO BRIDGE is painted bright blue to blend in with the San Diego Bay and the sky.

San Diego

Our tour begins at the southern part of the state, just over the Mexican border, with a visit to sunny San Diego and its nearby seaside towns. With brilliant blue skies, miles of sandy beaches, and a natural deep-water harbor, it's forever summer here! People find any excuse to enjoy life outdoors along, in, and over the chilly Pacific Ocean.

In 1904, the huge HOTEL DEL CORONADO ("the Del") gifted the nation with the first electrically lit, outdoor living Christmas tree. Before this, outdoor Christmas trees were decorated with candles.

The massive *USS MIDWAY*, docked at Navy Pier, was the longest-serving aircraft carrier, performing its patriotic duty from just after World War II through the Gulf War, and is now a floating museum.

At WRECK ALLEY, divers go deep underwater to explore huge ships sunk to create an artificial reef.

On a WHALE-WATCHING CRUISE, you may spot a CALIFORNIA GRAY WHALE, the state marine mammal. These migrating gentle giants travel more than 12,000 miles every year.

Who you calling a goldfish? The GARIBALDI is an orange-red damselfish that swims near the La Jolla caves. It may be named for Giuseppe Garibaldi, a 19th-century Italian soldier whose army wore red shirts into battle. The Garibaldi is the state's official marine fish.

Swab the decks on the *STAR OF INDIA*, the world's oldest active sailing ship (it survived a cyclone and a mutiny!), docked at the Maritime Museum of San Diego.

Stats and Facts

FAST FACTS

ABBREVIATION: CA

CAPITAL: Sacramento

STATEHOOD: September 9, 1850, 31st state

NUMBER OF COUNTIES: 58

POPULATION: About 40 million. One out of eight Americans lives in California. Almost two million more people live in California than in Canada!

AREA: 164,000 square miles. It's the third-largest state in total area.

The nickname THE GOLDEN STATE comes from the Gold Rush and from the fields of golden poppies, the state flower, that bloom in the spring.

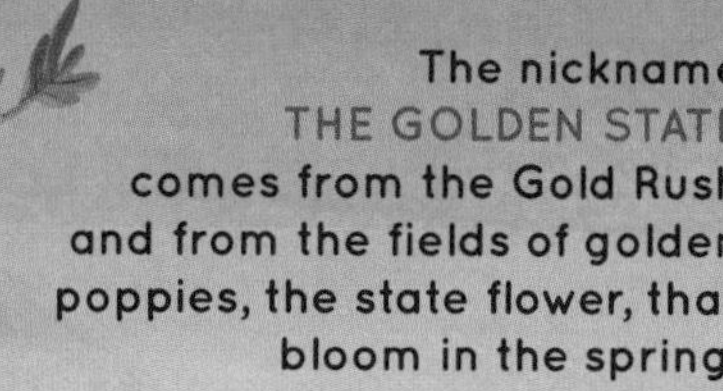

The state motto, "EUREKA!" (an ancient Greek expression that means "I have found it!"), refers to the discovery of gold in the Sierra Nevada mountain range. Eureka is also the name of a town in the northwestern part of the state.

The CALIFORNIA GRIZZLY BEAR on the state flag and seal is the official state animal. Before the Gold Rush brought thousands of people in the mid-1800s, the bears were plentiful. But by the 1920s, humans had killed them all off, and today California is the only state with an EXTINCT official state animal.

And that bear on the flag isn't some random grizzly. His name was Monarch, and he weighed an impressive 1,100 pounds. He was captured by Mount Gleason in 1889, as part of a publicity stunt by newspaper magnate William Randolph Hearst, and lived unhappily in captivity until his death in San Francisco 22 years later.

Next-Door Neighbors

NORTH: Oregon

WEST:

CALIFORNIA GOT ITS NAME BY MISTAKE

In the 1500s, a Spanish romance novel about a mythical island paradise called California was super popular. The island was ruled by a Black warrior queen named Calafia and filled with gold. When Spanish explorers sailed north from Mexico, they came across some land surrounded by water. They assumed it was an island, so they named it after the book they liked so much. Eventually, they discovered that the water was on only three sides, making it a peninsula. The peninsula became known as Baja California (Lower California), and the mainland was called Alta California (Upper California). And hundreds of years later, what do you think was discovered here? Gold!

IN THE NATION, CALIFORNIA HAS THE MOST:

- people
- language diversity (over 220 languages are spoken)
- acres of organic farmland
- national parks
- automobiles
- smog
- restaurants per person
- celebrities

STATE SUPERLATIVES

- Mount Whitney (14,500 feet) is the HIGHEST POINT in the lower U.S.
- Death Valley's Badwater Basin (282 feet below sea level) is the LOWEST POINT in the U.S. The lowest and highest points in the lower U.S. are both in California and only 80 miles apart!
- Salton Sea (227 feet below sea level) is the LOWEST LAKE in the U.S.
- Furnace Creek in Death Valley scorched the HIGHEST TEMPERATURE in North America with a sizzling 134 degrees Fahrenheit on July 10, 1913.
- At 20,105 square miles, San Bernardino County is the LARGEST U.S. COUNTY by area and is larger than nine states.
- Los Angeles County is the nation's MOST POPULOUS COUNTY—it has more people than 40 individual states!

Pacific Ocean SOUTH: Mexico EAST: Nevada and Arizona

Los Angeles

Lights! Camera! Sparkle! Get your cameras ready—we've rolled up to Los Angeles (also known as the Entertainment Capital of the World) in time for a star-studded event. During the day, you'll spot dozens of movies, TV shows, and online videos being filmed around the large city and on historic studio lots that you can tour. In the evenings, paparazzi's flashbulbs light up celebrities stepping out for glamorous premieres. So join in, wave to your fans, and strike a pose!

Colorful OLVERA STREET, the city's original main street and now a Mexican marketplace, is known as the birthplace of Los Angeles.

The FILM INDUSTRY started in New Jersey but moved to California to escape from the light-bulb inventor Thomas Edison's legal claims. The sunshine was a bonus!

At the ACADEMY AWARDS, also called the Oscars, movie stars walk the RED CARPET—except the carpet is really burgundy. It's a more flattering shade for pictures.

Oscar winners can't sell their TROPHY without first offering it back to the Academy for one dollar.

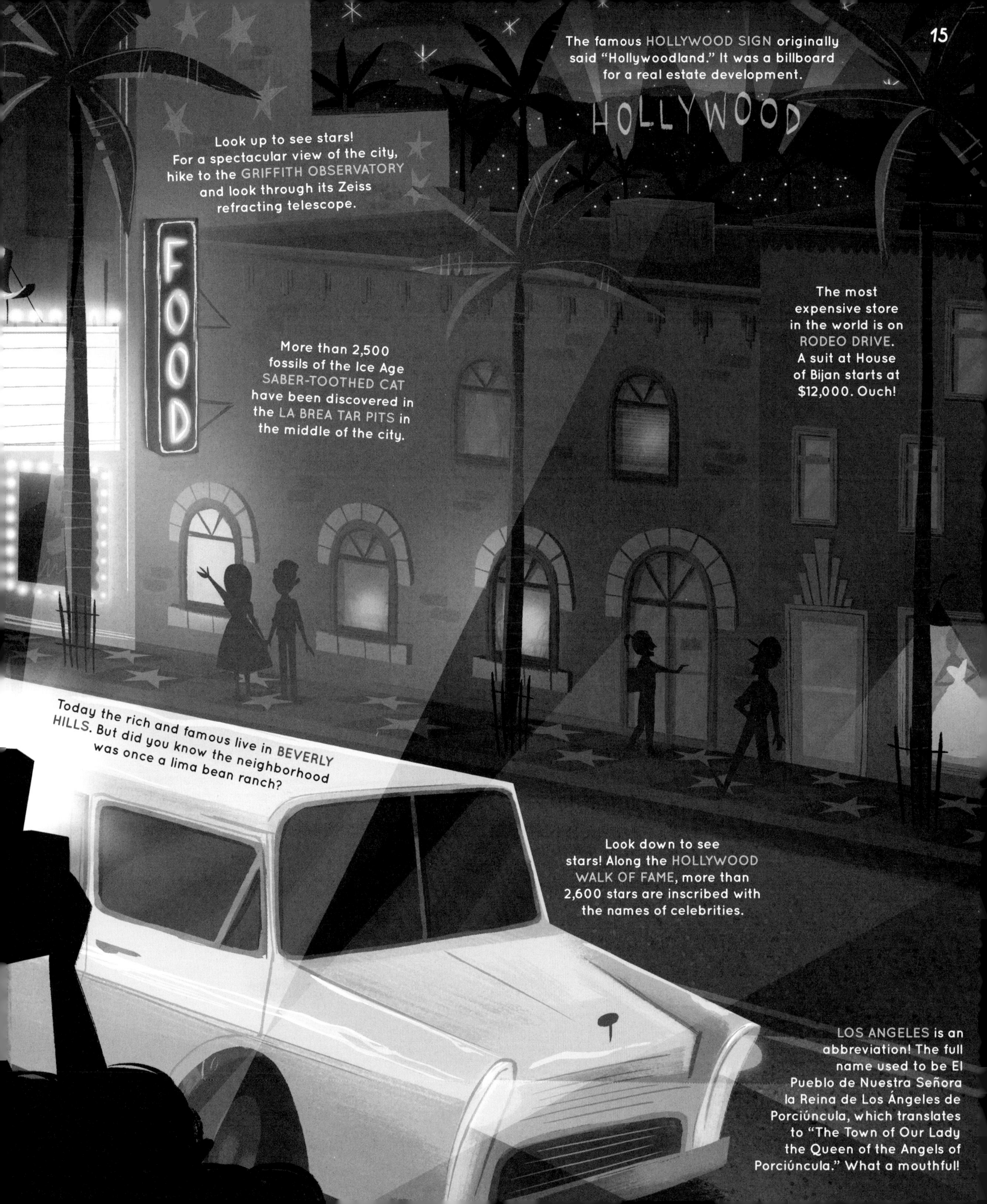

The famous HOLLYWOOD SIGN originally said "Hollywoodland." It was a billboard for a real estate development.

HOLLYWOOD

Look up to see stars! For a spectacular view of the city, hike to the GRIFFITH OBSERVATORY and look through its Zeiss refracting telescope.

FOOD

More than 2,500 fossils of the Ice Age SABER-TOOTHED CAT have been discovered in the LA BREA TAR PITS in the middle of the city.

The most expensive store in the world is on RODEO DRIVE. A suit at House of Bijan starts at $12,000. Ouch!

Today the rich and famous live in BEVERLY HILLS. But did you know the neighborhood was once a lima bean ranch?

Look down to see stars! Along the HOLLYWOOD WALK OF FAME, more than 2,600 stars are inscribed with the names of celebrities.

LOS ANGELES is an abbreviation! The full name used to be El Pueblo de Nuestra Señora la Reina de Los Ángeles de Porciúncula, which translates to "The Town of Our Lady the Queen of the Angels of Porciúncula." What a mouthful!

History Timeline

10,000 BCE Indigenous tribes call what is now California home. There are eventually more than 500 tribes, including the Cahto, Cahuilla, Chumash, Kumeyaay, Maidu, Miwok, Modoc, Mojave, Ohlone, Paiute, Pomo, Tolowa, Wintun, and Yuma.

1542 Juan Rodríguez Cabrillo, the first European to explore what is now California, sails into San Diego Bay, then up the Russian River, claiming the land for Spain. And what does Spain do? Nothing. For almost 200 years!

1579 Sir Francis Drake lands near Point Reyes, claiming that territory for England and naming it Nova Albion.

1849 The Gold Rush sparks large immigration from China. The nation's first-known Chinese restaurant opens in San Francisco. Many Irish immigrants, fleeing famine in Ireland, also arrive.

1850 California becomes the 31st state on September 9th.

1868 The University of California is established.

1869 First transcontinental railroad is completed, making travel to California easier. Over 14,000 Chinese laborers work under brutal conditions to lay tracks heading east.

1870s California becomes a major farming state, growing wheat at first, then citrus, grapes, vegetables, nuts, and more.

1890 Yosemite National Park is established.

1906 A massive earthquake shakes San Francisco.

1942-45 Japanese American citizens are imprisoned in internment camps. They didn't do anything wrong but were targeted based on their race and the unfounded fear they'd help the enemy.

1945 Sylvia Mendez's father files a lawsuit that will outlaw Mexican American segregation in California schools.

1955 Disneyland opens in Anaheim.

1962 Cesar Chavez and Dolores Huerta organize migrant farm laborers into a union.

1966 The Black Panther Party is founded in Oakland by Huey P. Newton and Bobby Seale to fight for political and economic equality. It later provided free breakfasts for children.

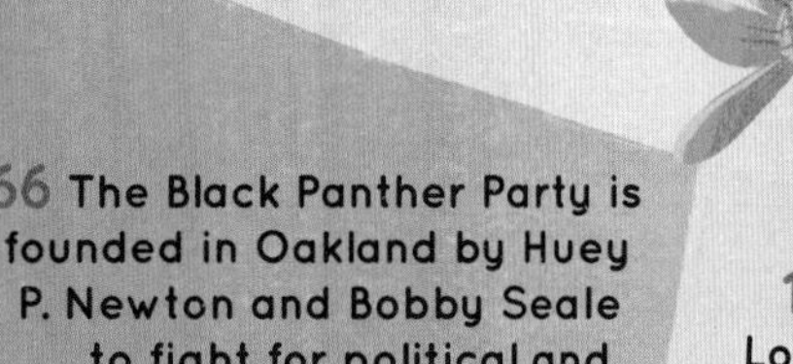

1967 The "Summer of Love" attracts hippies and musicians to the Haight-Ashbury section of San Francisco.

1974 U.S. president Richard Nixon resigns. The California native remains the only one to do so.

1769 Father Junípero Serra, a Franciscan priest, journeys from Mexico to San Diego to start the first of 21 coastal missions along the El Camino Real trail. The mission system is meant to convert the Native people to Christianity but results in the deaths of over a third of the Native population.

1776 The United States Declaration of Independence is signed.

1804 California's first orange grove is planted at Mission San Gabriel.

1821 Mexico wins its war against Spain for independence, and California becomes a Mexican territory.

1834 Mission system ends.

1846-48 Mexico and the U.S. go to war (mostly over who gets Texas). U.S. wins, and Mexico sells California and other territories to the U.S. for just $15 million dollars.

1848 James Marshall discovers gold at Sutter's sawmill in Coloma, kicking off the Gold Rush. 300,000 fortune seekers swarm in, harming Native populations and the environment.

1910 Angel Island opens as a point of entry to the U.S. for many immigrants. However, it also serves as a prison for hundreds of Chinese immigrants because the U.S. Congress passed an act in 1882 that barred Chinese immigration; that act wasn't overturned for 60 years.

1911 California grants women the right to vote.

VOTE

1927 The first movie with sound (called a talkie) is made in Los Angeles.

ENLIST NOW!

1930s During the Great Depression, thousands of Dust Bowl farmers move from the Plains to California.

1937 The Golden Gate Bridge opens in San Francisco.

1939 David Packard and Bill Hewlett start their computer company in a Palo Alto garage.

1941 The U.S. joins World War II after Japan bombs Pearl Harbor in Hawaii.

1978 San Francisco's Harvey Milk becomes California's first openly LGBTQ+ elected official (and one of the first in the country).

HARVEY MILK FOR SUPERVISOR

1976 Steve Jobs and Steve Wozniak start Apple Computers in Los Altos. Silicon Valley will soon become the world's center for computer innovation.

2004 *SpaceShipOne*, the first private crewed mission to space, lifts off from the Mojave Desert.

2020 California is the first state to order a lockdown during the global coronavirus pandemic.

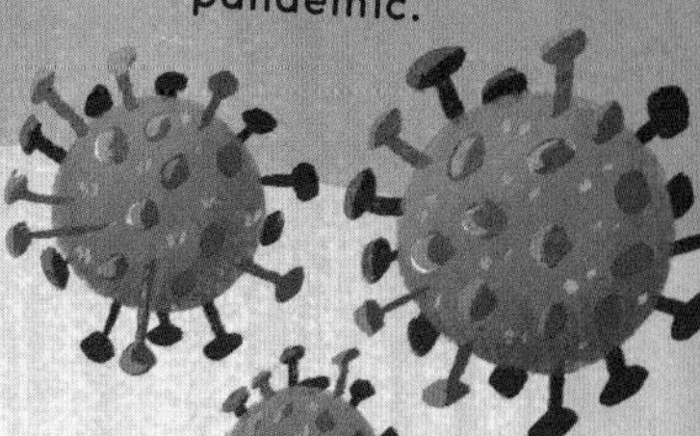

Central Valley

Hungry? Let's stop at one of the Central Valley's many fruit stands or at a pick-your-own farm for fresh farm-to-fork deliciousness. The Golden State grows over one-third of the nation's vegetables and two-thirds of its fruits and nuts—and most of that growing happens right here in the Valley's fertile farmland. Stretching 450 miles, the Central Valley is (yep, you guessed it) in the middle of the state and pancake-flat. The nutrient-rich soil, mild climate, cool ocean breezes, and almost 300 days a year of brilliant sunshine create perfect growing conditions. Avocados, strawberries, pistachios, apricots, plums . . . yum!

Thick white TULE FOG blankets the Valley on winter mornings. Drivers hate it because it makes the roads hard to see. Farmers love it because the fog shields young plants from sunlight and the condensation waters crops.

The Central Valley is really TWO VALLEYS: the San Joaquin to the south and the Sacramento to the north.

The ARTICHOKE is the state vegetable. Italian immigrants started growing artichokes in California in the late 1800s.

Central Valley farmers produce around 250 DIFFERENT CROPS. Over 90 percent of the nation's almonds, apricots, artichokes, broccoli, cauliflower, celery, figs, garlic, kiwifruit, nectarines, olives, persimmons, pistachios, plums, pomegranates, raisins, spinach, canned tomatoes, and walnuts are grown here.

FARM WORKERS come from Mexico, and other countries around the world, to plant, care for, and harvest the crops. Without them, the crops would never make it to our tables.

The SUNFLOWER is native to America. People have been using its seeds to make flour and clothing dye for over 500 years. Today it is grown mostly to produce cooking oil.

AVOCADOS! 2 for $5

Thirsty farmland needs water! In times of drought, Central Valley farms face WATER CHALLENGES. Can you guess the crops that drink up the most water? Alfalfa (cow feed), almonds, and pistachios.

Growing up during the Great Depression, young CESAR CHAVEZ and his Mexican American family were migrant workers, traveling from farm to farm in California. In the 1960s, Chavez and DOLORES HUERTA organized the workers into a labor union and led peaceful strikes, boycotts, and marches to bring about higher wages and improve conditions. The union later became known as the United Farm Workers of America (UFW).

Sports

Surfing is the official state sport, but outdoorsy locals can also be found running, sliding, gliding, and pedaling on the state's fields, trails, mountains, and courts.

California has been wild about SURFING since three teenage Hawaiian princes first rode redwood boards off the coast of Santa Cruz in 1885. Today, the bravest longboarders tackle 50-foot giant swells (taller than an apartment building!) at MAVERICKS near Half Moon Bay. Good thing the WET SUIT was invented in california!

At the annual DOG SURFING contest at Huntington Beach (also known as Surf City USA), hounds hop a curl and hang twenty. They're judged on swagger and length of the ride.

What do you get when you cross water-skiing with surfing? WAKEBOARDING! Tony Finn helped to start the sport in 1985 in San Diego with his invention of the "Skurfer."

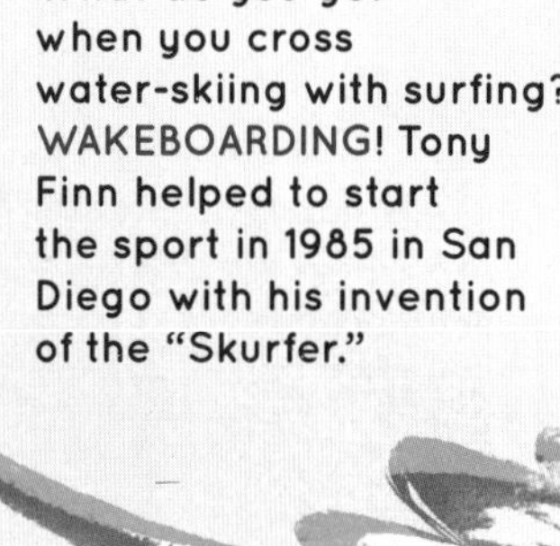

California has more MAJOR-LEAGUE PROFESSIONAL TEAMS than any state. See the last page in this book for a list of some of them. How many can you name?

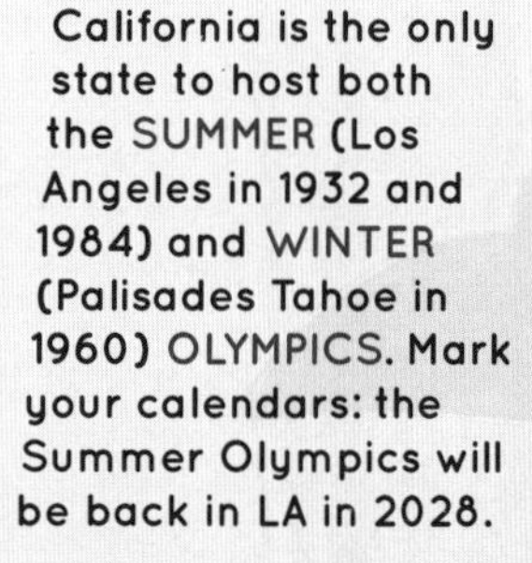

California is the only state to host both the SUMMER (Los Angeles in 1932 and 1984) and WINTER (Palisades Tahoe in 1960) OLYMPICS. Mark your calendars: the Summer Olympics will be back in LA in 2028.

Made popular by surfers who were bored (or "board"—get it?) when waves were tame, SKATEBOARDING was originally called sidewalk surfing. Kick flip and ollie in San Diego's skate parks every May 29 to celebrate TONY HAWK, the first boarder to complete a 900-degree aerial rotation.

TENNIS mega-superstar sisters Serena and Venus Williams served their first aces on public courts in Compton with their dad as their coach.

In 1948, Santa Monica held the first-ever BEACH VOLLEYBALL competition with a prize—a case of Pepsi!

Hands in the air! The first recorded full-stadium WAVE was during a playoff game between the Oakland A's and the New York Yankees at the Oakland Coliseum in 1981.

BMX (bicycle motocross) sped into action after SoCal kids began racing their bikes on dirt tracks to imitate their motocross heroes.

MOUNTAIN BIKING was born when a group of teens in the early 1970s rode single-speed balloon-tire bikes along the rugged terrain of Mount Tamalpais in Marin County.

California native SOCCER superstars Landon Donovan and Alex Morgan have set scoring records for the U.S. national teams. Landon started playing at age 5, but Alex didn't begin until 14.

MASCOTS make game day super fun(ny)! Some of the state's quirkiest cheerleaders are:

Boltman (SD Chargers)
Cecil the Sagehen (Pomona College/Pitzer College)
Chuck the Condor (LA Clippers)
Lou Seal/Luigi Francisco Seal (SF Giants)
Peter the Anteater (UC Irvine)
Rampage (LA Rams)
Sammy the Banana Slug (UC Santa Cruz)
San Diego Chicken (SD Padres)
SJ Sharkie (San Jose Sharks)
Sourdough Sam (SF 49ers)
Stanford Tree (Stanford University)
Stomper the Elephant (Oakland Athletics)
Wild Wing (Anaheim Ducks)
Willie the Wave (Pepperdine)

Eighty-foot-tall MCWAY FALLS is one of only two waterfalls in the state to flow directly into the ocean during high tide. The other is Alamere Falls in Marin County.

UNDERWATER KELP FORESTS provide a home to over 1,000 sea creatures. Unlike trees, kelp don't have roots but use clawlike holdfasts to grip hard surfaces.

The MONTEREY BAY AQUARIUM was used as inspiration for the movie *Finding Dory*. Visit to touch live bat rays and sea stars!

When BOTTLENOSE DOLPHINS sleep, they shut down only half of their brain—and the opposite eye. The other half of the brain stays awake, alert for predators and obstacles.

BIXBY BRIDGE, one of the world's highest single-span bridges, was built by prisoners from San Quentin State Prison in exchange for time off their jail sentences.

The village of CARMEL-BY-THE-SEA has no street addresses, so giving directions sounds something like, "third cottage after the big blue house two blocks from the center of town."

To keep from drifting out to sea when resting and eating, groups of 10 to 100 SEA OTTERS float side by side and form a raft by wrapping themselves in strands of kelp.

The goofy-looking NORTHERN ELEPHANT SEAL can hold its breath underwater for up to two hours. And when a huge male gets angry, his bulbous nose inflates like a balloon!

Big Sur

Now, this is California dreamin'! Peaceful Big Sur, masked by mist or bathed in sunshine, offers up the drama—rugged bluffs, towering cypress trees, crashing surf, remote beaches, majestic marine life and tide pools. It's no wonder the magical Central Coast has attracted and inspired naturalists, artists, and musicians for years.

Trees & Flowers

Wood you believe that California is home to more plant species than any other state? At least one-third of its native plants are found nowhere else in the coun-*tree*!

A BRISTLECONE PINE almost 5,000 years old (that's older than the Egyptian pyramids) is the world's oldest living organism. Its location is kept top secret to protect it—all we know is it's somewhere in the Inyo National Forest.

GENERAL SHERMAN is the name of the largest living single-stem tree by volume. The GIANT SEQUOIA is 275 feet tall and over 36 feet in diameter at the base. Some of its branches are larger than most full-sized trees growing east of the Mississippi.

The CALIFORNIA FAN PALM is the only palm tree native to the state. In 1931, Los Angeles planted more than 25,000 super tall and skinny Mexican fan palms. These trees only live 75 to 100 years and aren't great for climate change (they don't fight pollution, give shade, or provide fruit you can eat), so the city is replacing them with native trees as they die out.

The bright orange CALIFORNIA POPPY is the state flower. Called Copa de Oro ("cup of gold") by early Spanish settlers, Indigenous people used it to treat toothaches and headaches.

The end of the NAVEL ORANGE looks like a belly button! First grown in Riverside in the 1870s, the juicy, seedless fruit caused the state's "second gold rush"—but this time the gold was sweet citrus.

No flower says Christmas like the POINSETTIA. At one point, the Ecke Ranch in Encinitas grew more than 90 percent of all poinsettias (also called lobster flower and flame-leaf flower) purchased in the U.S.

At the beginning of the SoCal summer and again in the fall, JACARANDA TREES bloom a riot of purple-blue flowers. That sticky stuff on the petals may look like sap, but it's the poop of aphids feasting on the flowers' nectar!

The leaves of native CALIFORNIA YARROW have such a strong, bitter odor that one of its nicknames is "old man's pepper." You can use yarrow to stop a nosebleed!

Help monarch butterflies by planting MILKWEED in your garden. For two weeks of their life cycle, monarch caterpillars must munch milkweed leaves to transform into chrysalises and then orange-and-black butterflies. In the winter, migrating monarchs often stop in Pismo Beach.

MONKEY FLOWERS have funny-face blossoms that look like grinning monkeys. They are pollinated by hummingbirds.

The hot-pink PRICKLY PEAR CACTUS is almost entirely edible (just make sure to remove all the spines first). The pads are used to make nopales, and the tangy fruit is mashed into jam and even ice cream.

Many of California's over 40 native species of SUCCULENTS are called live-forevers because they last for up to 100 years in the wild. Not quite forever, but close.

San Francisco

Grab your camera! We're pulling up to the most photographed bridge in the world: the Golden Gate Bridge, connecting the vibrant city of San Francisco to Marin County. The bridge may look red, but it's actually orange (the paint's name is International Orange). The U.S. Navy had wanted it to be gray or black-and-yellow-striped; however, once architect Irving Morrow saw the steel with the red-orange primer (the first coat of paint), he liked how it complemented the blue-gray San Francisco Bay, blended with the golden hills, and stood out in the morning fog. Way to go, Irving!

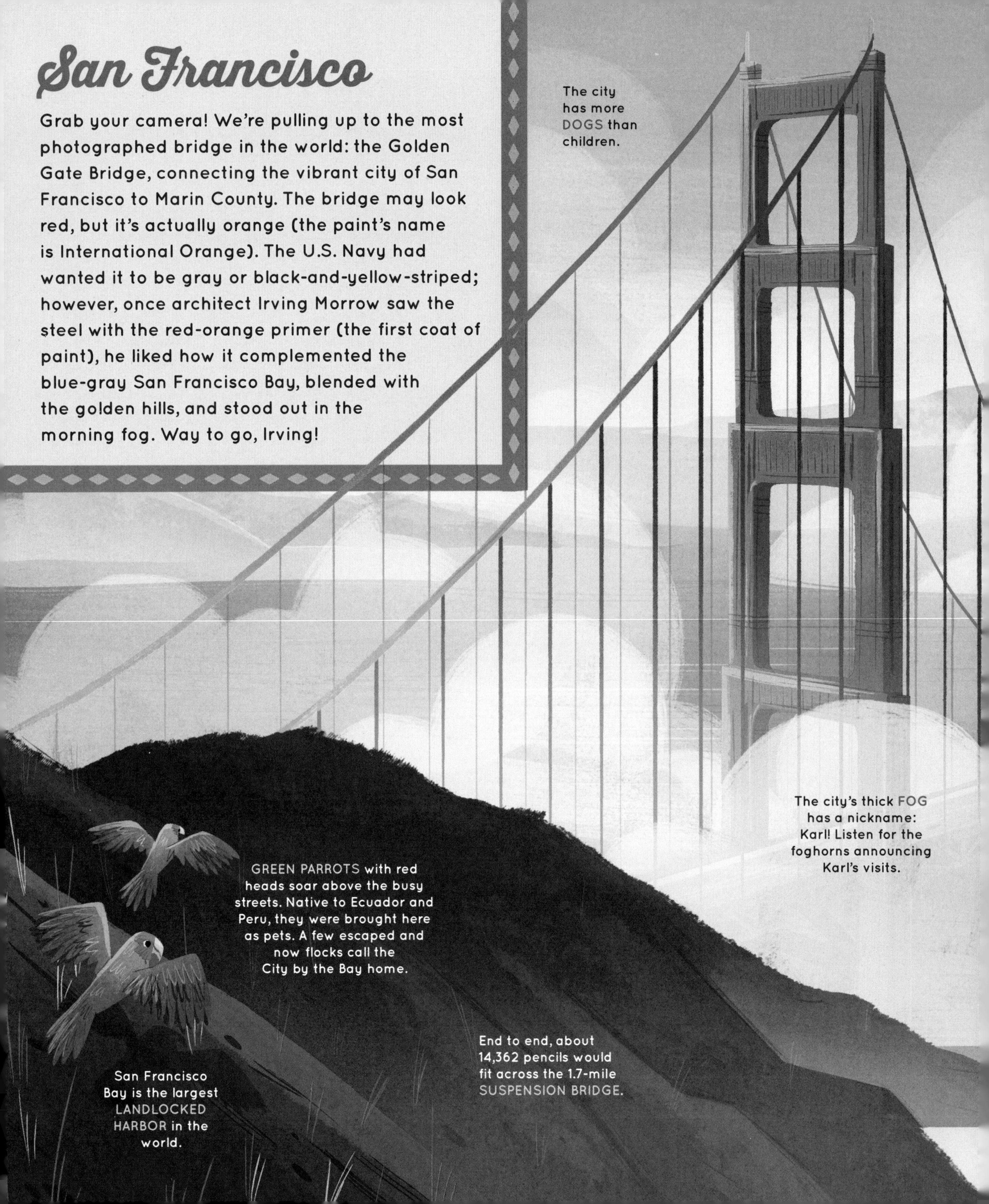

The city has more DOGS than children.

The city's thick FOG has a nickname: Karl! Listen for the foghorns announcing Karl's visits.

GREEN PARROTS with red heads soar above the busy streets. Native to Ecuador and Peru, they were brought here as pets. A few escaped and now flocks call the City by the Bay home.

End to end, about 14,362 pencils would fit across the 1.7-mile SUSPENSION BRIDGE.

San Francisco Bay is the largest LANDLOCKED HARBOR in the world.

CABLE CARS were built in 1873 to go up and down the city's many steep hills. One of San Francisco's first Black female streetcar conductors was 16-year-old Maya Angelou before she became a celebrated poet.

Could you escape from ALCATRAZ? The infamous island prison housed some of the country's most dangerous criminals, including gangster Al Capone.

Living on the dock of the bay . . . In charming Sausalito, quirky and luxury HOUSEBOATS provide floating homes for many families.

The Golden Gate Bridge can act as a THERMOMETER! It's made of steel, so it expands and contracts with temperature changes, causing the roadway to rise and fall up to 16 feet.

San Francisco's CHINATOWN on Grant Avenue started in 1846, making it the oldest in North America.

Some say the fog makes the city's SOURDOUGH BREAD taste so great. Not sure that's true, but the bread does date back to the Gold Rush, when traveling miners carried sourdough starter with them so they'd always be able to bake fresh bread.

Pee-uw! The stink of guano, or bird poop, coming off the FARALLON ISLANDS, west of the Golden Gate Bridge, can be smelled from ships over a half-mile away. More than 300,000 seabirds nest on the rocky islands.

A herd of BISON roams in the middle of GOLDEN GATE PARK! The first bison were brought here in the 1890s, as a symbol of the Wild West.

Slip on a costume and join pink-gorilla mascot Ape Hashbury at the BAY TO BREAKERS race, running from the Embarcadero across to where the breaking waves crash into Ocean Beach.

Museums & Attractions

What's better than high-flying thrills at amusement parks and curious exhibits at museums? When they're amplified by the quirky and unusual!

Physicist Larry Shaw started the celebration of March 14 as "Pi (π) Day" at the EXPLORATORIUM science museum in San Francisco. The first digits of pi, a long, never-ending number, are 3.14.

Let the sun shine! The PACIFIC WHEEL on Santa Monica Pier is the world's first solar-powered Ferris wheel.

The GIANT DIPPER on Santa Cruz's boardwalk is the state's oldest roller coaster. When it opened in 1924, it cost only 15 cents to ride!

In the early days of the Pirates of the Caribbean ride at DISNEYLAND in Anaheim, real human skeletons from UCLA's medical center were used as props—but not anymore! Did you know that Disneyland employees have secret code words? "Code V" for a "protein spill" is announced when some kid on the spinning teacups vomits.

Don't count sheep—count penguins! Experience your own night at the museum with a wild sleepover at the CALIFORNIA ACADEMY OF SCIENCES in San Francisco.

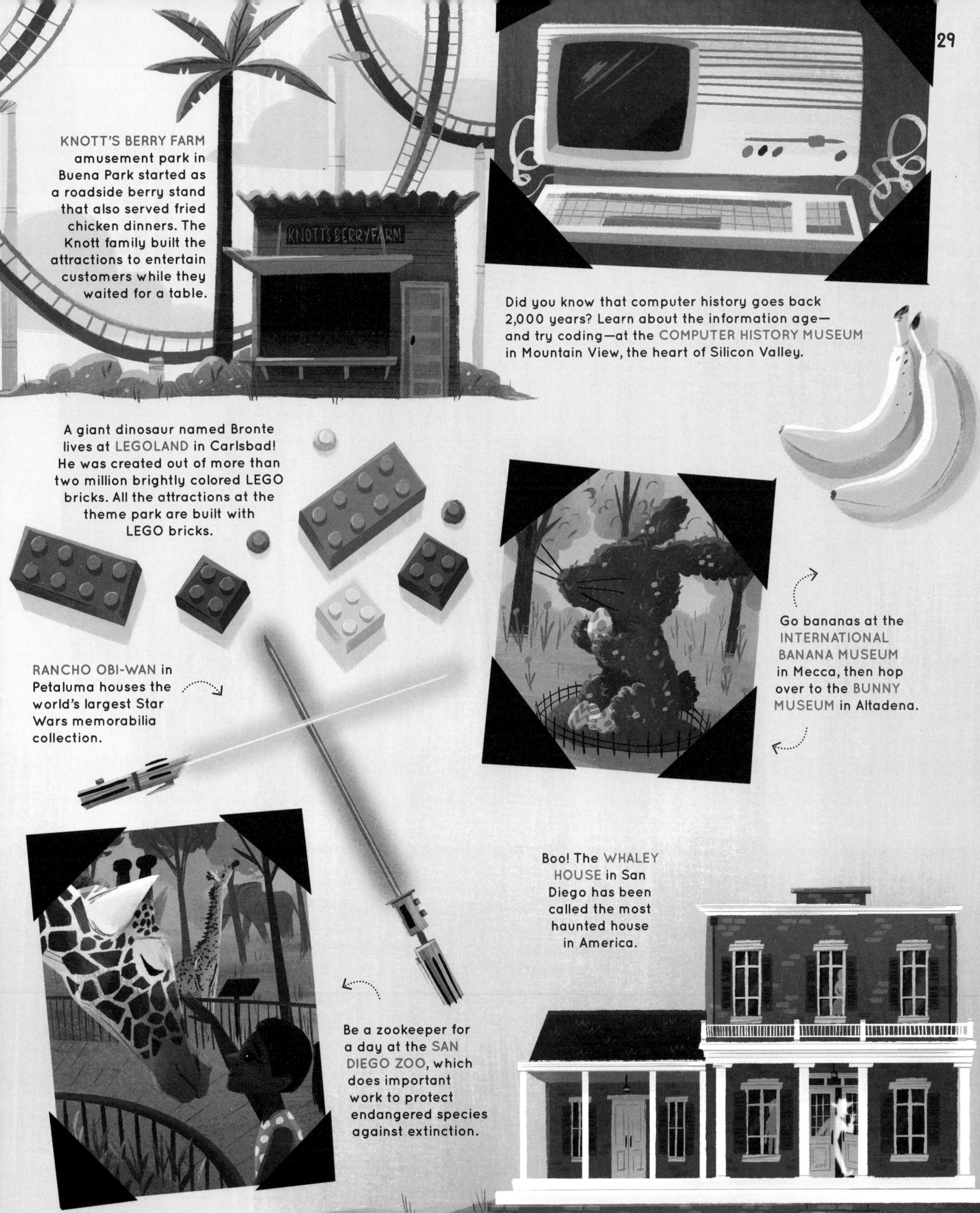

KNOTT'S BERRY FARM amusement park in Buena Park started as a roadside berry stand that also served fried chicken dinners. The Knott family built the attractions to entertain customers while they waited for a table.

Did you know that computer history goes back 2,000 years? Learn about the information age—and try coding—at the COMPUTER HISTORY MUSEUM in Mountain View, the heart of Silicon Valley.

A giant dinosaur named Bronte lives at LEGOLAND in Carlsbad! He was created out of more than two million brightly colored LEGO bricks. All the attractions at the theme park are built with LEGO bricks.

Go bananas at the INTERNATIONAL BANANA MUSEUM in Mecca, then hop over to the BUNNY MUSEUM in Altadena.

RANCHO OBI-WAN in Petaluma houses the world's largest Star Wars memorabilia collection.

Boo! The WHALEY HOUSE in San Diego has been called the most haunted house in America.

Be a zookeeper for a day at the SAN DIEGO ZOO, which does important work to protect endangered species against extinction.

Grapes are a type of BERRY and come in red, purple, black, blue, pink, or green.

The grapes you eat are TABLE GRAPES, and they're larger and have thinner skin and fewer seeds than WINE GRAPES.

There were once more than 300 STONE-ARCH BRIDGES in the Napa Valley.

A RAISIN is a dried grape.

Napa & Sonoma

Up, up, and away! We're about to float through the sky in a colorful hot-air balloon for a bird's-eye view of the Napa and Sonoma Valleys. Here, grape vineyards cover the sprawling, rolling countryside. This area north of San Francisco is one of the most well-known wine-growing regions in the world (in addition to France, Italy, and Spain). Sunrise is the best time for a balloon ride, and the beautiful, lush valleys glow in the golden light.

The wine industry began here not long after the Gold Rush, but it was Franciscan missionary Father Junípero Serra who planted the state's FIRST GRAPES in 1769, to make wine for the church.

A CHASE CREW follows a hot-air balloon in a chase vehicle. The crew coordinates with the pilot on a radio to figure out where it will land. Because of the wind, the landing spot is different every time!

A sheep, a duck, and a rooster were the first live passengers to fly in a HOT-AIR BALLOON, in 1783 in France. They were totally fine—except the sheep kicked the rooster mid-flight! Today, take a ride in the sky during the Sonoma County Hot Air Balloon Classic.

During harvest time, jump into a barrel of freshly picked grapes and stomp them with your BARE FEET. In olden times, this was how grapes were crushed into juice. Today, a press is used.

Food Glorious Food

California is all about fresh ingredients, and its most famous dishes reflect the diverse groups who've made the state their home.

Two SUSHI chefs from Los Angeles and one from Canada all claim to have created the CALIFORNIA ROLL in the 1970s. They rolled imitation crab, cucumber and avocado in seaweed, and put the sticky rice on the outside—suddenly everyone was craving sushi!

Guac out! AVOCADO on a sandwich instantly transforms it into a "California sandwich." The creamy green fruit was introduced from Mexico, but in the late 1920s, mail carrier Rudolph Hass planted an avocado seedling in his backyard in La Habra Heights. The tree produced a new, tasty variety that he named after himself. (I mean, wouldn't you?)

Sugar rush! Ghirardelli chocolates, Abba-Zaba chewy taffy, and See's square lollipops are classic California candies. In 2012, See's Candies licked the record for the world's largest LOLLIPOP, weighing in at a sweet 7,003 pounds.

Fans eat more than 2.5 million hot dogs, including the 10-inch-long DODGER DOG, each season, making Dodger Stadium the top hotdog seller in Major League Baseball.

Late one night in 1937, Bob Cobb, owner of the Brown Derby Restaurant in Hollywood, pulled leftover lettuce, avocados, tomatoes, chicken, hard-boiled eggs, bacon, and cheese from the fridge—and his COBB SALAD was so delicious, it was added to the menu.

El Salvadorian PUPUSAS are thick, handmade corn tortillas filled with cheese, chicharron, and beans, and are served with a side of curtido (pickled cabbage slaw).

You get to cook thin strips of BULGOGI and other yummy grilled meats right on your table at Korean BBQ restaurants.

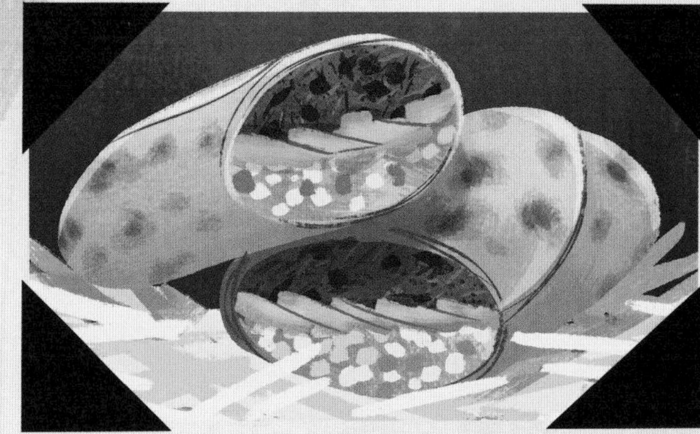

Tiny Balboa Island is known for FROZEN BANANAS dipped in chocolate and rolled in nuts.

San Diego's mouthwatering CALIFORNIA BURRITO has a secret ingredient: French fries! Rice and beans take center stage in San Francisco's massive foil-wrapped MISSION BURRITO.

Like condiments with a fiery kick? At the Huy Fong factory in Irwindale, 100 million pounds of chili peppers are used every year to make SRIRACHA and other hot sauces. TAPATÍO, produced in Vernon, was created by a Mexican immigrant who couldn't find any "good" hot sauces in California.

Italian immigrant fishermen used to gather on the San Francisco wharfs and cook leftovers from their catch (Dungeness crabs, scallops, calamari, mussels, fish, and clams) into a tomato-based seafood stew called CIOPPINO.

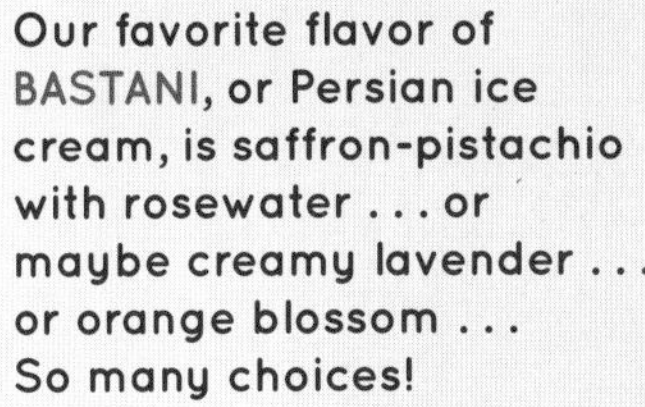

Our favorite flavor of BASTANI, or Persian ice cream, is saffron-pistachio with rosewater . . . or maybe creamy lavender . . . or orange blossom . . . So many choices!

Legend has it, a Gold Rush prospector came into the El Dorado Hotel in Hangtown (now called Placerville) and demanded the most expensive meal. The cook whipped up the wacky HANGTOWN FRY by scrambling an egg with oysters and bacon.

Spoiler alert: FORTUNE COOKIES aren't from China. It's believed Japanese immigrant Makoto Hagiwara started them by handing out cookies with thank-you notes tucked inside at the Golden Gate Park Japanese Tea Garden in San Francisco in the 1890s.

The fun is on the inside when you bite into a XIAO LONG BAO, or soup dumpling. Visit the San Gabriel Valley for some of the most authentic XLBs.

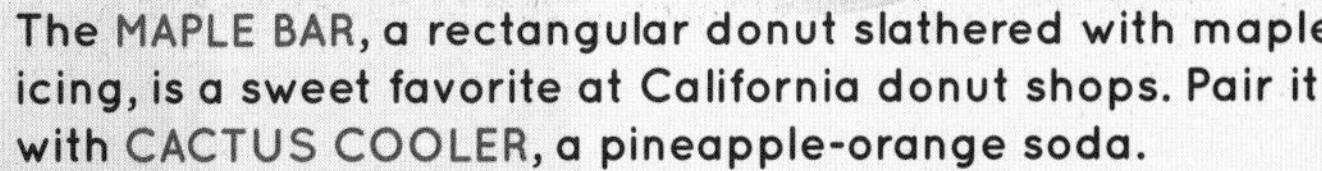

The MAPLE BAR, a rectangular donut slathered with maple icing, is a sweet favorite at California donut shops. Pair it with CACTUS COOLER, a pineapple-orange soda.

Redwood Forests

We're cruising up the North Coast and—whoa!—look up. Way, way up! Giants are out there. Giant coast redwood trees, that is. They're the tallest trees on the planet, reaching incredible heights of 350 feet (that's the same as 20 giraffes standing on top of one another!). Hyperion in Redwood National and State Parks is the world's tallest living tree, at around 380 feet.

Environmental activist Julia Butterfly Hill climbed a redwood and lived up there for 738 days to PROTEST a lumber company's destruction of the ancient trees. She succeeded, saving three acres of trees from the loggers.

REDWOODS AND SEQUOIAS are gigantic, ancient trees. Coast redwoods grow taller, but sequoias have thicker trunks.

Redwoods drink almost 40% of their water from the dense coastal FOG.

Redwoods' incredibly thick, cinnamon-color BARK contains natural chemicals that shield them against the triple threat for trees: insects, fungi, and fire.

Icy-cold Smith River was declared the CLEANEST RIVER in the U.S. (except for Alaska), and it's the last undammed river in California.

The HUMBOLDT'S FLYING SQUIRREL uses a parachute-like membrane to glide from tree to tree.
Ever dreamed of living inside a tree? The ONE LOG HOUSE, hollowed out of a single redwood log in 1946, looks like a mobile home with living, dining, and bedroom areas.
I got you! Redwoods live in GROVES, so their shallow, widespread roots can intertwine, literally holding one another down during strong winds and floods.
The towering trees have itsy-bitsy PINE CONES!
The 1,100-pound ROOSEVELT ELK, the largest mammal living in the redwood forests, was named after President Theodore Roosevelt.
The first redwoods appeared over 240 million years ago, during the time of the DINOSAURS—and way before humans existed.
CLIMATE CHANGE WARRIORS! Through photosynthesis, coast redwoods capture more carbon dioxide (CO_2) emitted from fossil fuels than any other tree on Earth.
Steven Spielberg filmed parts of the movie *The Lost World: Jurassic Park* at FERN CANYON, one of California's only rain forests in Redwood National and State Parks.

Animals

California has such a range of different landscapes and climates, so it makes total sense it boasts not only the most animal species but also the most endemic (meaning not living anywhere but here) species. Meet a few of our favorite feathered, furry, and creepy-crawly friends.

Now, that's a hairdo! California's state bird, the CALIFORNIA QUAIL, sports a topknot that looks like a single feather but is actually a cluster of six overlapping plumes.

The CALIFORNIA CONDOR, the largest flying bird in North America, has a wingspan up to 10 feet long (the length from the floor to the ceiling in most rooms). The critically endangered scavenger needs to flap its wings only once an hour while it glides!

CALIFORNIA NEWTS have flame-fighting superpowers! When exposed to a wildfire, the slime coating on the newt's skin foams up and transforms into a crusty white ash, protecting it from catching fire.

TULE ELK, the smallest elk in North America, were recently brought back from the brink of extinction. About 5,700 tule elk now roam the grasslands of Point Reyes National Seashore and other California state parks.

ILLACME PLENIPES, the world's leggiest MILLIPEDE, is kickin' it in central California. Although "milli" means one thousand, they have up to 750 legs (most other millipedes have an average of just 62 legs). Talk about false advertising.

What's the difference between a MOUNTAIN LION, a PUMA, and a COUGAR? Trick question! They're all names for the same big cat found in the state's deserts, snowy mountains, and even some remote backyards. These wild cats can jump 15 feet high and sprint up to 50 miles per hour.

Are zebras black with white stripes or white with black stripes? Turns out, they're black animals with white stripes. There's a herd of wild ZEBRA along Highway 1 in San Simeon! William Randolph Hearst, the newspaper tycoon who built Hearst Castle, brought zebras from Africa as part of his large private zoo in the 1920s. After Hearst died in 1951, the zebras were left to graze free on the hillside overlooking the Pacific Ocean.

And they're back! According to legend, CLIFF SWALLOWS flock to Mission San Juan Capistrano every March 19 (St. Joseph's Day) to build their nests. On October 23 (St. Juan's Day), they circle the ruins of the Great Stone Church before flying off for their winter migration.

The ANNA'S HUMMINGBIRD eats more insects than any other North American hummer. Their tiny wings beat super fast—about 40 to 50 times per second! Hummingbirds are the only birds that fly backward!

The mayor of the mountain town of Idyllwild is a GOLDEN RETRIEVER! Every weekend, Mayor Max II (full name: Maximus Mighty-Dog Mueller II) wears a tie and sits in his pickup truck to take meetings with the townspeople.

The CALIFORNIA DOGFACE BUTTERFLY is the official state insect. Can you spot the poodle-like face silhouette on the wings of the male? The female is solid yellow with a black dot on each wing.

The Ahwahneechee, part of the MIWOK people, have built cone-shaped bark houses in Yosemite to honor their ancestors and reclaim the home where they'd once lived for thousands of years.

WATERMELON SNOW is a real thing! Microscopic algae with a special pigment turns snow on the highest mountains light pink during summer. But, like with yellow snow, don't eat it!

The rare SIERRA NEVADA RED FOX was spotted in the park in 2014 after not being seen there for almost 100 years. There may be only 18 to 39 left in North America!

Yosemite National Park

Everything in Yosemite National Park is supersized—giant waterfalls, giant granite walls, giant valleys, giant sequoia trees, giant meadows. The enormous park within the Sierra Nevada mountains is basically the size of Rhode Island! In 1864, President Abraham Lincoln signed the Yosemite Valley Grant Act, which protected 39,000 acres of Yosemite Valley and Mariposa Grove. Even though Yosemite wasn't the first national park (it's #3), it was the first area of land set aside by the government for preservation and protection. And that's a big deal!

The immense curved horns of the SIERRA NEVADA BIGHORN SHEEP are made of keratin, the same material as our fingernails.

The peaks of El Capitan and Half Dome are playgrounds for climbers. Sacramento-born Alex Honnold was the first climber to FREE SOLO (climb without any ropes) the 3,000-foot rock face of El Capitan, in 2017.

Moises and Daniel Monterrubio, two brothers from San Francisco, set the park record for LONGEST HIGHLINE when they walked a 2,800-foot-long nylon rope over a gully 1,600 feet below in 2021.

Hiking to the top of YOSEMITE FALLS, one of the world's tallest waterfalls, is like taking the stairs to the top of the Empire State Building—twice.

The GIANT SEQUOIAS in Mariposa Grove, some of the biggest trees on Earth, have seeds the size of a flake of oatmeal.

Mountaineer GALEN CLARK is believed to be the first person to count and measure the giant sequoias here. He'd hike through the park barefoot, because shoes were "cruel and silly instruments of torture."

See a RAINBOW AT NIGHT! If the sky is clear, the light from a full moon can produce rainbows from a waterfall's mist. They're known as lunar rainbows or moonbows.

About 85% of the WATER people in San Francisco drink is snowmelt piped in from Yosemite National Park.

Before the National Park Service was established in 1916, Yosemite was patrolled by the BUFFALO SOLDIERS, regiments of Black infantrymen on horseback, who chased down poachers and timber thieves, and extinguished forest fires.

Inventions

Dream big in the Golden State and embrace the new, the incredible, and the never-been-seen-before. Here are just a few of the many inventions from innovative California.

How sweet! Retired San Diego schoolteacher Eleanor Abbott invented the board game CANDYLAND in 1948 while she was in the hospital recovering from polio and wanted something fun to do.

Brothers Paul and Jim Van Doren started VANS in Anaheim in 1966, and SoCal skateboarders loved the way the rugged shoes' sticky waffle soles gripped their boards. The idea for the black-and-white checkerboard pattern came from watching skaters color their shoes with black pens.

The RAINBOW FLAG, a symbol of LGBTQ+ pride and hope, was designed by San Francisco artist Gilbert Baker in 1978. He sewed the first one by hand.

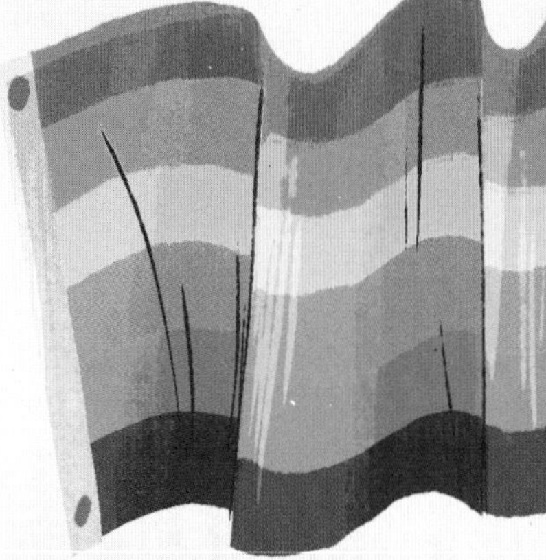

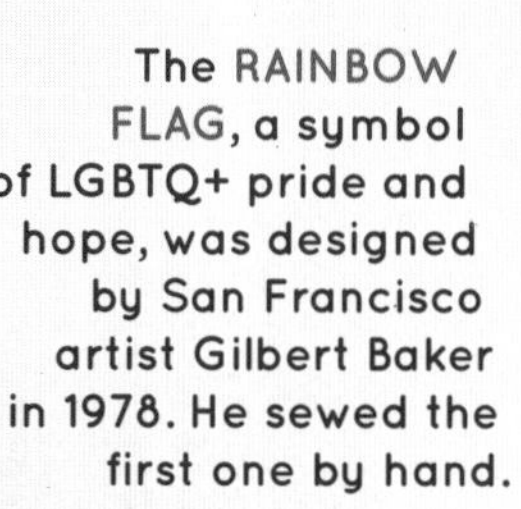

Frank ZAMBONI invented the first ice-resurfacing machine in Paramount in 1949. Before his machine, it took four workers over an hour to clean and resurface the ice-skating rink he owned.

When Eric Yuan created ZOOM video conferencing, he had trouble at first convincing investors to fund his business, because they didn't think it would be a success!

Googol

SEARCH

Search engine GOOGLE, created by computer scientists Larry Page and Sergey Brin in 1999, was named after a googol, which is the number 1 followed by 100 zeros.

IN-N-OUT was car-dependent California's first drive-through burger stand when it opened in 1948 in Baldwin Park. Ssssh! In-N-Out has a secret menu. Locals order their burger or fries "animal style."

The first MCDONALD'S was a barbecue restaurant started by brothers Richard and Maurice McDonald in San Bernardino in 1940. The EGG MCMUFFIN breakfast sandwich was invented in Santa Barbara in 1971 by franchise owner Herb Peterson.

When Joseph Friedman saw his daughter struggle trying to drink a milkshake out of a straight straw, he invented the BENDY STRAW in San Francisco in 1937.

DORITOS were invented at Disneyland to use up stale food! The park's Mexican(ish) restaurant would take the stale tortillas, then spice and fry them into triangular chips. Frito-Lay started producing Doritos ("little golden things" in Spanish) in 1966.

In 1905, eleven-year-old Frank Epperson from San Francisco invented the POPSICLE when he left a fruit drink with a stirrer outside in the cold overnight. He originally called his frozen treat Epsicle.

The modern window-cleaner helper, the SQUEEGEE (the most fun name to say!), was invented in 1936 by Italian immigrant Ettore Steccone in Oakland.

Levi Strauss and tailor Jacob Davis created the first pair of BLUE JEANS in 1873 by stitching canvas together and adding brass rivets. To prove their ruggedness, Strauss hooked up two horses to a pair to try to tear them apart. DENIM is the state's official fabric.

Bill Winkenbach created the first FANTASY FOOTBALL LEAGUE in 1962 with some friends. It was called the Greater Oakland Professional Pigskin Prognosticators League (GOPPPL), and Oakland Raiders star George Blanda was the first player selected.

Los Angeles entrepreneur and Mattel cofounder Ruth Handler invented BARBIE in 1959. She named the doll after her daughter, Barbara. Can you guess her son's name? Ken!

In 1856 (before railroads and telephones), San Francisco was cut off from the country by the Sierra Nevada. A Norwegian immigrant nicknamed SNOWSHOE THOMPSON came to the rescue. He carried mail across the mountains on skis!

The WASHOE people used the lakeshore as their sacred summering grounds, calling it "Da ow a ga" (meaning "edge of the lake"). It's believed early settlers garbled the first two syllables, so the lake became known as "Tahoe."

Lake Tahoe contains an average of 37 trillion gallons of FRESH WATER. There's enough water to supply everyone in the U.S. with 50 gallons per day for five years!

The lake loses much of its water to EVAPORATION. If you could gather the water that evaporates from the lake every 24 hours, it would supply the daily requirements of the entire city of Los Angeles.

Lake Tahoe is one of the world's CLEAREST lakes.

Watch your toes! Legend has it, a Loch Ness Monster-type creature named TAHOE TESSIE lives in the lake.

Can you be in TWO PLACES at once? Lake Tahoe can! About two-thirds of the lake is in California and one-third is in Nevada.

If you were stranded on a remote mountain, what would you do to survive? Donner Pass, north of Lake Tahoe, was named for the DONNER PARTY, a wagon train of 87 settlers who were trapped by snow during the winter of 1846-47. Freezing and starving, a few survived by eating their fellow travelers!

South Lake Tahoe averages about 34 feet of SNOW a year—enough to cover a three-story building! In the 1850s, miners slid down the peaks on 15-foot-long skis. Today there are hundreds of SKI TRAILS.

The thick bark of the tall JEFFREY PINE trees smells like vanilla, butterscotch, or pineapple.

The lake's only native fish is the LAHONTAN CUTTHROAT TROUT. The name "cutthroat" comes from the streaks of red beneath its jaw.

In the winter, the WHITE-TAILED JACKRABBIT sheds its gray-brown fur and turns entirely white.

Lake Tahoe

We've arrived at one of California's most popular playgrounds: Lake Tahoe. Do you want to (a) swim and paddleboard in the glimmering, clear waters; (b) ski and snowboard down the snowcapped peaks; or (c) hike in the towering pine forests? We say: (d) all of the above, please! The largest alpine lake in North America, Lake Tahoe sits high in the Sierra Nevada mountains. What are you waiting for? Let's play!

Fun Festivals

California is overflowing with festivals that are both head-scratchers and totally awesome (and sometimes a bit of both). From pillow fights to jumping frogs to garlic ice cream, there's something for everyone.

Is Bigfoot real? Find out at the BIGFOOT DAZE FESTIVAL in Willow Creek, which calls itself the Bigfoot Capital of the World. There have been many reported sightings of the legendary hairy apelike monster (also called Sasquatch) in the nearby woods.

Enter your mega-sized pine cone in the World's Largest Pine Cone Contest (Coulter pines and sugar pines only, please) at the PINE CONE FESTIVAL in Running Springs.

For a *toad*-ly hoppy time, bring your frog to the CALAVERAS COUNTY FAIR AND JUMPING FROG JUBILEE in Angels Camp. Rosie the Ribiter is the frog to beat—she jumped 21 feet, 5.75 inches in 1986.

Pucker up for lemon pie-eating contests at the CHULA VISTA LEMON FESTIVAL and the GOLETA LEMON FESTIVAL. No hands allowed, so dive in to the tart gooeyness face-first! California grows most of the nation's lemons.

These funny-looking pups (many of them are rescues) at the WORLD'S UGLIEST DOG CONTEST at the Sonoma-Marin Fair in Petaluma are so doggone cute!

Petal power! The TOURNAMENT OF ROSES PARADE held on New Year's Day in Pasadena has a strict rule: every inch of every float must be covered with flowers or other natural materials. An estimated 18 million flowers are used!

It's scratching time at the annual POISON OAK SHOW in Columbia. Compete for best bouquet (think flower arranging except with poison oak) and worst-looking rash. We're itchy just thinking about it!

Do you have strong enough vocal cords to win the Howling Contest at the COULTERVILLE COYOTEFEST? Howlers are judged on loudness and most authentic coyote howl.

Every summer, the town of Kenwood hosts the WORLD PILLOW FIGHT CHAMPIONSHIP. Contestants balance on a greased metal pole set over a mud-filled pit and let the feathers fly!

For a large dose of holiday cheer, drive down CHRISTMAS TREE LANE in Altadena, where almost one mile of Deodar cedar trees twinkle with colorful lights. It's reported to be the nation's oldest large-scale outdoor Christmas display.

Bring a breath mint (or two) to the GILROY GARLIC FESTIVAL for the garlic fries, garlic jelly, and garlic ice cream. Stinky fact: California produces 90% of the nation's garlic crop.

Sacramento

"Sac," "Sactown," and "City of Trees" are just a few of the many nicknames of state capital Sacramento, but "River City" best describes where it is. When gold was discovered in the Sierra Nevada foothills, wannabe miners rushed to the area, and many sailed inland from San Francisco on the Sacramento River. But once they reached where the Sacramento River and the American River met, they got off their boats and built trading posts and a town. And Sacramento was born.

In 1860, Sacramento was one of the birthplaces of the PONY EXPRESS, a horseback-relay mail-delivery service that ran more than 1,800 miles between California and Missouri. It lasted only 18 months before the telegraph took over.

Sacramento Kings' fans set the world record in 2013 for LOUDEST CROWD.

The CROCKER ART MUSEUM is the oldest public art museum west of the Mississippi River.

Stop and smell the roses at the INTERNATIONAL WORLD PEACE ROSE GARDENS in State Capitol Park—there are over 140 varieties of roses to choose from!

The CAPITOL BUILDING in the capital (alert: that's a homophone!) looks like Washington D.C.'s stunt double. The gold-plated copper ball on top of the dome symbolizes the Gold Rush.

The only city in the world with more TREES than Sacramento is Paris, France.

A feral black cat nicknamed SENATOR CAPITOL KITTY lived at the Capitol for 13 years (1991-2004). You can visit her grave near the south entrance.

Sure, you know Sacramento is the STATE CAPITAL, but did you know it wasn't the first choice? In fact, it was one of six cities that has served as the state capital. The others were Monterey, San Jose, Vallejo, Benicia, and San Francisco.

The bright yellow TOWER BRIDGE crosses the SACRAMENTO RIVER, the longest river entirely within California. The bridge was originally silver but repainted yellow-gold to match the gold Capitol dome.

Say cheese! The city's famous SQUEEZE BURGER wears a melted cheese "skirt!"

California produces about 80% of the world's ALMONDS. At the Blue Diamond Innovation Center in Sacramento, food scientists come up with tasty new ways to use almonds. Any ideas?

Climb aboard the CALIFORNIA STATE RAILROAD MUSEUM, the country's largest railroad museum. In 1863, the nation's first transcontinental railroad, connecting the Atlantic coast with the Pacific coast, broke ground in Sacramento.

The original city can be found UNDERGROUND. In 1862, an intense storm caused massive flooding that submerged the entire city underwater. When the city was rebuilt, the streets were raised one story, creating spaces and tunnels underground.

Change Makers

Countless creative and courageous Californians have left their mark and transformed our world. We are featuring just a handful of the state's influential thinkers, pioneers, artists, activists, athletes, and leaders. Many were the first from their community to achieve a goal, effect change, or do something super cool.

In 2021, KAMALA HARRIS made history as the first female, first Black, and first Asian American vice president of the United States. Born in Oakland, she was the first Black district attorney of San Francisco and the first Black U.S. senator from California before moving to the White House.

When Stockton-raised activist DOLORES HUERTA saw all the hungry farm children in the 1950s, she decided to help organize farm workers to fight for better conditions. She cofounded the United Farm Workers (UFW) and organized the 1965 Delano strike of 5,000 grape workers.

Growing up in Oakland, filmmaker RYAN COOGLER was thrilled when the clerk at a local comic book store introduced him to Black Panther, a superhero who looked like him. Coogler brought the world of Wakanda to life in his blockbuster movie *Black Panther.*

The youngest person to win all four top awards at the Grammys in one year (2020), BILLIE EILISH, along with her brother Finneas O'Connell, wrote and recorded their hit music in their Los Angeles childhood bedrooms.

Basketball legend KAREEM ABDUL-JABBAR learned his signature skyhook move in grade school, long before he took to the court for UCLA and the Los Angeles Lakers. He was the first NBA player to score more than 38,000 points.

The first Hispanic American female astronaut to go to space and the first Hispanic American director of NASA's Johnson Space Center, DR. ELLEN OCHOA, who grew up in La Mesa, logged close to 1,000 hours in space.

BRIDGET "BIDDY" MASON was enslaved when she arrived in Los Angeles in 1851, and by the time she died free in 1891, she'd become one of the city's first Black real estate moguls and one of its wealthiest women.

Born with an actual hole in his heart, snowboarding champion and San Diego native SHAUN WHITE had to have multiple operations as a kid. Already an impressive skateboarder, he switched to snowboarding at age six and won three Olympic gold medals and set the record for most X Games snowboarding gold medals.

Born and raised in Los Angeles, AMANDA GORMAN was only 19 years old when she was named the first National Youth Poet Laureate, and in 2021, she read her poem "The Hill We Climb" in front of the nation at the U.S. presidential inauguration.

After moving to California for graduate school and settling in Westmoreland, DALIP SINGH SAUND became the first Asian American, first Indian American, and first Sikh American to take office in the U.S. Congress in 1957.

MISTY COPELAND was raised by a single mother in a motel room in San Pedro and didn't take her first ballet lesson until age 13. In 2015, she made history when she became the first Black female principal dancer at American Ballet Theatre.

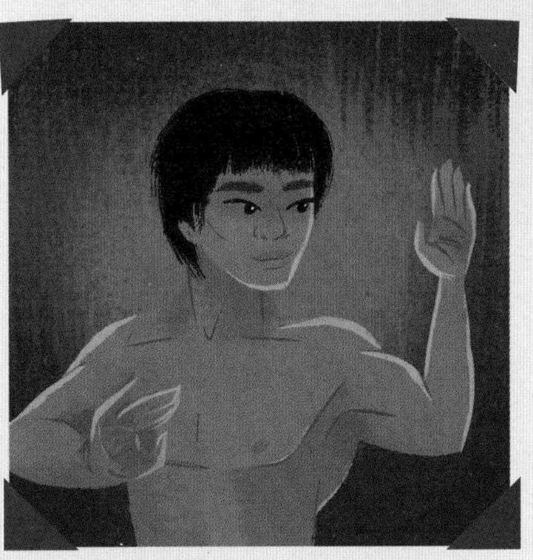

San Francisco-born actor BRUCE LEE revolutionized the sport of mixed martial arts, creating his own style, Jeet Kune Do, which he described as "the art of fighting without fighting."

DR. KAZUE TOGASAKI, who survived the Great San Francisco Earthquake of 1906 and during World War II endured the Japanese American internment camps, was one of the first Japanese American women to earn a medical degree in the U.S. She delivered over 10,000 babies during her career!

Known as the Mother of Balboa Park, horticulturist KATE SESSIONS turned the San Diego park green by planting hundreds of trees. She introduced bougainvillea, the jacaranda tree, poinsettias, and birds-of-paradise to the state.

JOSHUA TREES are found in nearby JOSHUA TREE NATIONAL PARK, straddling the Mojave and Colorado Deserts. The twisted trees provide a home for lizards, insects, and birds.

Superstrong whirlwinds called DUST DEVILS can spin up in the sands.

Shine an ultraviolet light on GIANT DESERT HAIRY SCORPIONS, and a chemical makes them glow in the dark!

KANGAROO RATS are like tiny ninjas, leaping as high as nine feet in the air to avoid snake attacks.

Recognize Tatooine? Two of the STAR WARS movies were filmed in Death Valley.

Death Valley

Bring plenty of water—we're heading into Death Valley in the Mojave Desert, near the Nevada border. Legend has it that the valley got its name after a group of gold miners in the mid-1800s unwisely used the parched land as a shortcut and got lost, and one traveler didn't make it out alive. No surprise there, as Death Valley is North America's lowest, hottest, and driest point. (Then again, the Timbisha Shoshone people survived here just fine for hundreds of years.) We're visiting at night as the sands cool down and the nocturnal animals wake—a time when the desert feels most alive.

The Awe of Mother Nature

Earthquakes, wildfires, floods, droughts, landslides, and volcanoes: Mother Nature likes to go wild in California. But no matter what scary hazard is thrown their way, locals know the secret to staying safe: be prepared. They create plans with their families, gather supplies, pack emergency kits . . . 'cause keeping that California-cool vibe is easy when you're ready for anything.

On Shaky Ground

Every day EARTHQUAKES rock the Golden State. Almost all are so tiny you never feel them. The earth shakes when pressure builds up on fault lines (where two large sections of Earth's crust, called tectonic plates, touch). One of the world's largest is the SAN ANDREAS FAULT, a crack that stretches for 800 miles across the state from the Salton Sea to Cape Mendocino.

Some scientists say Los Angeles and San Francisco could end up as next-door neighbors one day (because the tectonic plates are always moving), but that would take at least 15 MILLION YEARS to happen.

The GREAT SAN FRANCISCO EARTHQUAKE OF 1906 was the first natural disaster to be widely photographed. Over 80% of the city was destroyed—less from the shaking and more from fires that burned afterward. It took San Francisco nine years to rebuild.

Make Room in the Ark, Noah!

The GREAT FLOOD OF 1862, the largest flood in the recorded history of California, started after it rained for about 45 days and the rivers overflowed. The Central Valley turned into a sea, drowning 200,000 cattle and washing away thousands of farms. The city of Sacramento was submerged underwater, and adobe brick buildings in the southern part of the state melted into muddy piles.

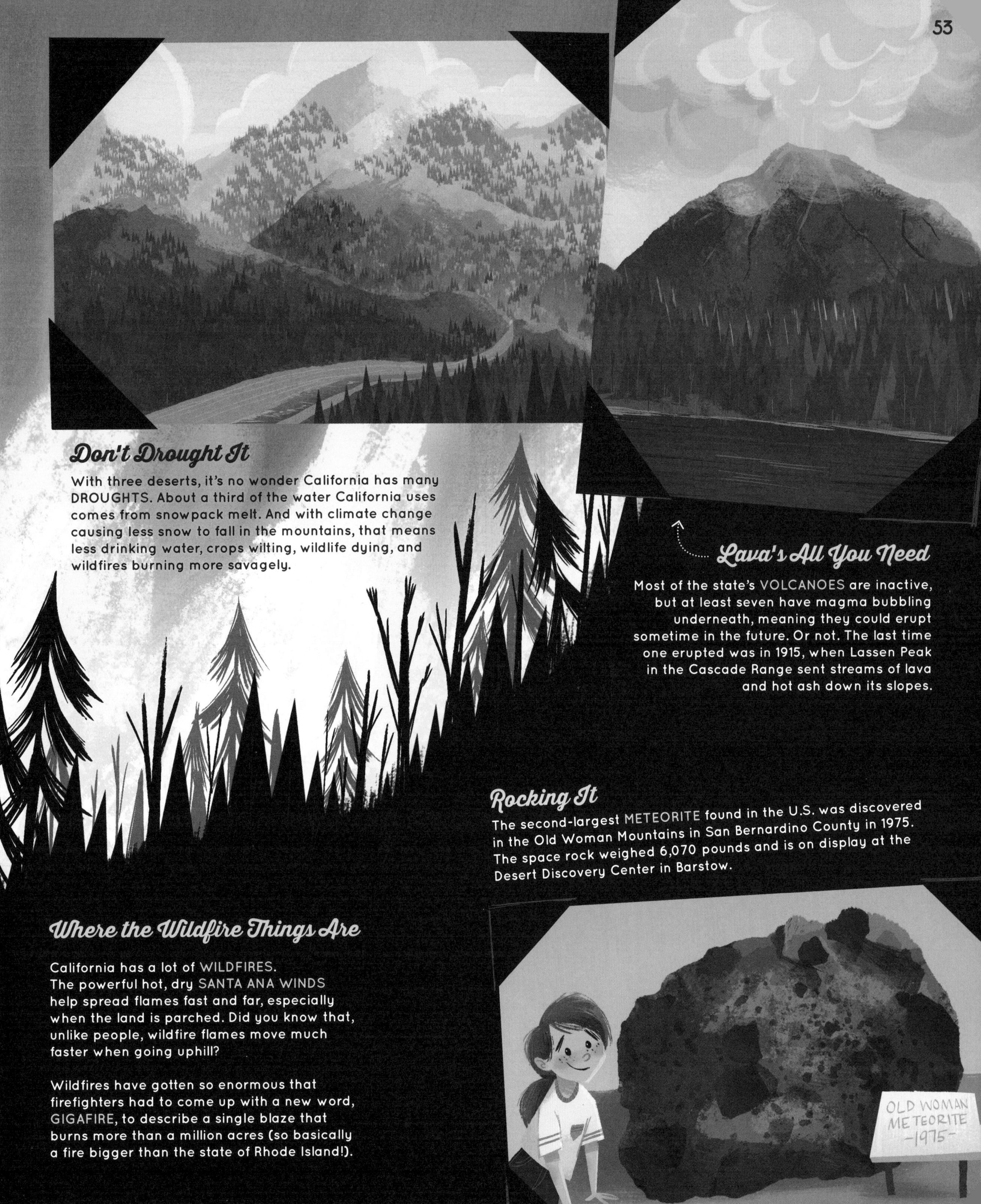

Don't Drought It

With three deserts, it's no wonder California has many DROUGHTS. About a third of the water California uses comes from snowpack melt. And with climate change causing less snow to fall in the mountains, that means less drinking water, crops wilting, wildlife dying, and wildfires burning more savagely.

Lava's All You Need

Most of the state's VOLCANOES are inactive, but at least seven have magma bubbling underneath, meaning they could erupt sometime in the future. Or not. The last time one erupted was in 1915, when Lassen Peak in the Cascade Range sent streams of lava and hot ash down its slopes.

Rocking It

The second-largest METEORITE found in the U.S. was discovered in the Old Woman Mountains in San Bernardino County in 1975. The space rock weighed 6,070 pounds and is on display at the Desert Discovery Center in Barstow.

Where the Wildfire Things Are

California has a lot of WILDFIRES. The powerful hot, dry SANTA ANA WINDS help spread flames fast and far, especially when the land is parched. Did you know that, unlike people, wildfire flames move much faster when going uphill?

Wildfires have gotten so enormous that firefighters had to come up with a new word, GIGAFIRE, to describe a single blaze that burns more than a million acres (so basically a fire bigger than the state of Rhode Island!).

Palm Springs

We're at the end of our wacky tour, and it's fry-an-egg-on-the-sidewalk hot! Luckily, we've splashed down in Palm Springs. Dive into one of over 50,000 different pools—there are more pools per person in this sunbaked desert vacationland than anywhere else in the country. Since the 1920s, Hollywood's movie stars have traveled to the Coachella Valley resort towns (over 300 days of sunshine a year here!) to play golf and tennis, hike up to canyon waterfalls, and lounge on pool floats. Last one in the water is a fried egg!

Sip a supersweet frosty DATE SHAKE while doing the backstroke! The Coachella Valley produces more than 90% of the country's dates. Dates grow on date palm trees and go back 50 million years to the Middle East.

Snap that perfect dino-selfie with Mr. Rex and Dinny, the famous gigantic steel-and-concrete roadside CABAZON DINOSAURS.

Tee up for the PALM DESERT GOLF CART PARADE and watch the tricked-out carts roll by. There are more than 100 golf courses in the area.

Celebrities sometimes check into hotels using an ALIAS, or fake name, to avoid unwanted attention. Johnny Depp once was "Mr. Drip Noodle." What would your alias be?

Why did MOVIE STARS choose Palm Springs? In the 1930s, Hollywood actors under contract weren't allowed to travel more than two hours away from Los Angeles. Hello, Palm Springs! A getaway one hour and 50 minutes from LA!
Thousands of giant, three-bladed wind turbines (the locals call them WINDMILLS) on wind farms create enough energy to power hundreds of thousands of homes in the Coachella Valley.
Why do so many houses in Palm Springs look the same? The flat roofs, geometric design, and big glass windows were part of an architectural style popular during the 1940s–1960s called MID-CENTURY MODERN.
The PALM SPRINGS AERIAL TRAMWAY's tram-car ride from the desert floor to San Jacinto Peak is one of the steepest ascents in the world.
Did you know that Palm Springs has a WALK OF STARS honoring actors, architects, musicians, and some U.S. presidents?
Frank Sinatra's former Twin Palms Estate has a PIANO-SHAPED SWIMMING POOL. What shape would you choose?

Weird, Weirder, Weirdest

California can be super weird when it wants to, and sometimes fabulous stuff doesn't neatly fit into any one category. But that's kind of the definition of quirky, right? So we've gathered all the oddness together!

Year after year, the CENTENNIAL LIGHT BULB glows at the Livermore-Pleasanton Fire Department. The exact same bulb has been burning since 1901.

It's a wild ride at the BRING YOUR OWN BIG WHEEL RACE down steep, curvy Vermont Street in San Francisco. While Lombard Street is famous for its zigzag turns, Vermont Street is actually the MOST CROOKED STREET in the city.

BUBBLEGUM ALLEY in San Luis Obispo is exactly what it sounds like: an alley covered with chewed bubblegum of all colors and flavors. It got its first glob of gum back in the 1950s.

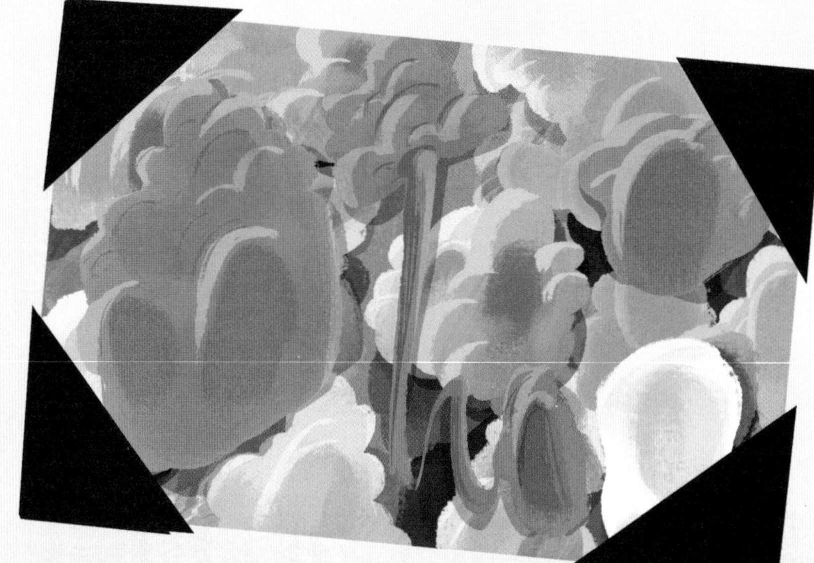

POTATO CHIP ROCK at Mount Woodson near San Diego looks just like the snack food!

The pretty PAINTED LADIES—a row of seven colorful Victorian houses in San Francisco—have starred in over 70 films and commercials, including the opening of the TV show *Full House*.

California has a chemical element named after it. CALIFORNIUM is a radioactive metal used to start up nuclear reactors.

In 1900, a law made it illegal to bury dead bodies in San Francisco, so cemeteries moved to nearby COLMA. With 17 cemeteries (and one pet cemetery) in this small town, the dead outnumber the living 1,000 to 1!

A GIGANTIC BEAR SCULPTURE named Ursa Mater (or Penny Bear) in Tahoe City is made out of 200,000 pennies. Can you do the math? That's a $2,000 bear!

There's an EGG VENDING MACHINE at Glaum Egg Ranch in Aptos with singing and dancing robotic chickens!

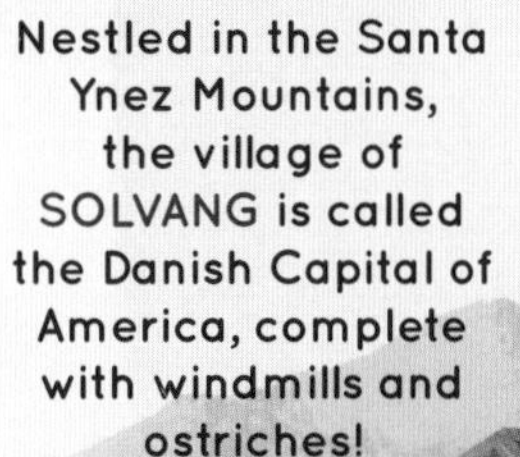

Nestled in the Santa Ynez Mountains, the village of SOLVANG is called the Danish Capital of America, complete with windmills and ostriches!

A massive TOOTH OF A MEGALODON (a prehistoric shark thought to be three times larger than a great white) was discovered in the Santa Cruz Mountains. A shark in the mountains? Yep, ten million years ago these mountains were all underwater.

1,680 jelly beans are made per second at the JELLY BELLY FACTORY in Fairfield. President Ronald Reagan (once governor of California) kept a bowl of them in his office and said he could tell a lot about a person by the flavor they picked.

This BIG state has several LARGE roadside attractions:

Artichoke—Castroville
Box of Raisins—Kingsburg
Chess Set—Morro Bay
Clam—Pismo Beach
Dinosaurs—Cabazon
Donut—Inglewood
Hammer—Eureka
Hamster Wheel—Point Loma
Lemon—Lemon Grove
Olive—Lindsay
Paper Cup—Riverside
Sewing Needle—Sacramento
Thermometer—Baker

Index

N.

O.

P.

R.

S.

U.

V.

W.

X.

Y.

Z.

Major-League Professional Sports Teams

National Football League
LA Chargers, LA Rams, SF 49ers
Major League Baseball
LA Angels, LA Dodgers, Oakland Athletics, SD Padres, SF Giants
National Basketball Association
Golden State Warriors, LA Clippers, LA Lakers, Sacramento Kings
Women's National Basketball Association
LA Sparks
Major League Soccer
LA Galaxy, LA FC, San Jose Earthquakes
National Women's Soccer League
Angel City FC, San Diego Wave FC
National Hockey League
Anaheim Ducks, LA Kings, San Jose Sharks